THE COLLEGE R.E.B.O.O.T.

THE COLLEGE R.E.B.O.O.T.

*6 Timeless Principles for
Reducing Student Loan Debt*

TAMEKA L. WILLIAMSON

THE COLLEGE R.E.B.O.O.T.
Copyright © 2021 Tameka L. Williamson
All rights reserved.

Published by Publish Your Gift®
An imprint of Purposely Created Publishing Group, LLC

No part of this book may be reproduced, distributed or transmitted in any form by any means, graphic, electronic, or mechanical, including photocopy, recording, taping, or by any information storage or retrieval system, without permission in writing from the publisher, except in the case of reprints in the context of reviews, quotes, or references.

Printed in the United States of America

ISBN: 978-1-64484-524-0 (print)
ISBN: 978-1-64484-525-7 (ebook)

Special discounts are available on bulk quantity purchases by book clubs, associations and special interest groups. For details email: sales@publishyourgift.com or call (888) 949-6228.
For information log on to www.PublishYourGift.com

Also by Tameka Williamson

Parents, Send Your Child to College for Free

Getting A Full Ride

A Road to Success: The College Planning and Preparatory Guide

Her Chronicles: Stories of Faith, Fear, and Fortitude (collaboration)

Teens & College Students: Outliving Their Expectations (collaboration)

TABLE OF CONTENTS

Acknowledgments ix

Introduction 1

Reexamine Your Motives and Goals 13

Educate Your Base on Your WHY 23

Begin with the End in Mind and Work Backwards 33

Outline Your Steps Forward 41

Orchestrate the Right Dream Team 53

Track, Monitor, and Control the Journey 61

R.E.B.O.O.T. the Road to Transformation 69

About the Author 75

ACKNOWLEDGMENTS

A hodgepodge of experiences, engagements, conversations, coaching sessions, and trainings (as well as the multiple roles I've been fortunate to occupy) helped mold the ideas and wisdom shared in this book. Having written multiple other books and technical research papers, this is likely one of my proudest accomplishments. That is because I get the opportunity to highlight a small segment of clients and their accomplishments to be used as a role model for other families on how to kill the college game and win.

I am indebted to my clients for trusting me as their coach over the years; it has been a privilege and indeed an honor. In sharing their stories, I have masked their identities to respect their confidentiality. Additionally, a good coach always learns from their clients. I want to thank them for teaching me and for making me and the program better for families in the years ahead. This book is for you, and may your successes help others succeed and afford them the opportunity to live their best lives.

Of course, I would be remiss if I did not mention my family and my support system. It's an absolute blessing to know that people don't necessarily have to be blood to be considered family. In addition to my wonderful parents, grandmother, great aunt, close colleagues, and boss, my tribe consists of some fairly incredible people. Please know how grateful I am for all of you and your unconditional love, accountability, support, lessons, and mentorship. I love and appreciate each of you. You know who you are.

I also cannot ignore the fact that God is my rock and my forever ride and die. He downloaded this book project and its chapters to me in a matter of hours, and gave me the words and resources to create it within a few days, even though it was a challenging time for our family. Thank you, Lord, for always providing exceeding abundance in more ways than I could ever ask for.

Finally, a special thanks to my sweetie pie. You've been that support structure, covering, and encourager, and I am grateful that we get to do life together. I love you to the moon and back.

INTRODUCTION

Think about it for a moment. Visualize five, ten, or even fifteen years from now and into your child's future.

What does it look like?

What kind of adult do you hope they will become?

Now, based on that vision, what type of traits do they possess? What kind of heart do they have? What type of career are they in?

These are the kinds of questions we need to ask ourselves today, because the decisions made now will dictate whether or not your child has the propensity, training, and knowledge base to fulfill the vision you have for them.

Are you cultivating an entitled child who is surviving thinking that life offers them do-overs, and that opportunities just come with a snap of the fingers? Or have you challenged them to assess and analyze their decisions to see if they make sense and to question what their impact will be in the future?

Being a close witness to the college admissions process, I see the answer to these questions played out daily during my prospecting and client appointments. If you're wondering what I'm talking about, let me give you a few scenarios. Let's consider Adam B, for example. Adam approached me about helping his daughter gain admission to her dream school. After a series of questions, I quickly realized there wasn't much for me to do in this situation. The daughter's dream school, Spelman College, is a college that has a very targeted audience and a limited funding pattern. Like many families I encounter desiring the same school, their funding models don't meet the family's funding needs, but his words to me were, "Well, this is her dream school, so I'll do what's necessary to make it happen, even if I have to get a parent loan to make her dreams come true."

Another example I like to share is with a different family who took advantage of the school's payment plan option. Don't get me wrong: getting on a payment plan can make the bill more palatable, but it has to be something you can maintain comfortably. This family also involved the mother wanting her son to be able to attend his "dream school" so she can make his dreams come true. This led to her pulling $7500 out of her 401k to cover the down payment, and a monthly payment plan of $1,650. Please bear in mind this payment arrangement only took care of year one, it doesn't deal with the years to follow. So there's a good chance those numbers will increase, or that the mom's financial situation could change, among other scenarios. Not to mention: is she going to withdraw that large sum each year from her retirement? Does she even have enough in her retirement to sustain a yearly withdrawal equating to $37,500 (bear in mind that kids are taking on average five years to graduate)? Spending this money now, how are you supposed to live when it's time to retire? These are all the questions that come to mind that families don't consider, and they are questions that we must discuss. Decisions tend to be based on the "now", with no regard to whether or not it's a decision we could fulfill for at least five years without any issues. When it comes to loans, we are assuming that the same level of approval will happen each year. That is not the case, because Parent PLUS loans are determined based on credit, and this impacts the debt-to-income (DTI) ratio. We'll talk more about what's wrong with this picture.

Before I do that, I want to get something straight. Don't get me wrong: I am not judging families for wanting the best for their kids. I totally understand that. But, at what cost is it worth it? What lessons are we teaching our kids, as we're preparing them to make decisions on their own as responsible adults? What you want out of life requires work, sacrifice, and sweat equity. Making these decisions should not be based on emotions, a short-term, or temporary situation. We must think about the impact today, as well as five, ten, and fifteen years into the future. This level of thinking is how you critically analyze and assess whether or not a decision is a good or a bad one. These are also the things we must consider when it comes to how we're raising and developing our kids and the next generation after them. How is it going to benefit or impact them today, as well as in the future? Because the reality is that the more we get caught up in the emotional side of selecting a college or university, the greater the chance the entire family will end up with life crippling debt that places major limitations on the next 20, 30, and 50 years of our lives. It is time for us to stop the madness, reboot, and start over because we are in a state of emergency as a country. The time is now for us to reset and retrain our minds on how to do college and do it more responsibly.

> *Reboot: to restart (a computer) by loading the operating system; boot again. to produce a distinctly new version of (an established media franchise, as a film, TV show, video game, or comic book): The studio is rebooting Spider-Man.*

Or:

> *to make a change in (something) in order to establish a new beginning: She's rebooting her career. Lower interest rates are intended to reboot the economy.*

"Reboot." Dictionary.com Unabridged, Random House, 2021, www.dictionary.com/browse/reboot

Either way, *reboot* implies the need to remove the blue screen on our computers (essentially, our brains) and start fresh so the cache can be emptied and the cookies cleared. Approaching the college application process as it's been done for years is expired and is leading too many families to a life crippled by a ball and chain on the ankle, following them everywhere they go.

As a society, we have been programmed to pursue our desires, hopes, and dreams regardless of the cost. Couple that mentality with the fallacy of reality TV syndrome and the instantaneous benefits of technology (often referred to as the microwave effect), and it's clear that we are in a state of emergency. The removal of critically thinking through the process of planning and working to get from point A to point B has adversely affected families, and they will pay the cost for generations to come. How do we know this? The continual growth of student loan debt to over $1.7 trillion is one clue precipitated by this sample of behaviors.

Consider these very common scenarios:
- "My child only applied to their dream school(s). There were no other options and we just did what was necessary for them to go." (This can take the unfortunate form of Parent PLUS loans, retirement withdrawal, home equity loan, private loans, etc.)

- "My baby worked hard to make good grades and I want them to attend the school of their choice, no matter the cost."
- "I know this school is offering my child a better offer, but a "top name" institution is where they want to be. So I am just letting my child make the choice and we will make the sacrifice."
- "I couldn't make them apply for scholarships and I don't want them to graduate with a lot of debt. So I committed to either withdrawing $7500 from my retirement account and entering a payment plan of $1700 a month; taking out a Parent PLUS loan for $26,500 the first year and then we will figure out the remaining years; or applying for a home equity loan to cover the first two years and hopefully we'll get the money to cover the remaining years."

What happened to the era when we were willing to put things on layaway and work to pay it off? Or putting in the work to get what we want and earning our keep? For certain, technology has improved the speed at which we can make things happen and can deliver results faster than we ever thought possible, but it was never intended to circumvent the basic premise of seed and harvest.

The microwave opened the door to cooking food faster and saving us time. In life, it translates to the mindset of wanting and receiving our desires "right now" and "on demand." So, it would seem then, every aspect of life must follow suit. How many of us are spoiled by the *Quicker! Faster! Now!* movement? Here, a few examples:

- Amazon Prime 2-Day or Same Day Delivery (who has time for snail mail?)
- Google Fiber (no more dial-up!)
- emails (who mails letters anymore?)
- influencers with viral videos on TikTok (things like building and cultivating a platform, and networking and connecting with people over time takes too long!)
- TSA Pre-check/CLEAR (standing in long security lines is for amateurs!)
- ordering food via an app (I can do other things while my food is prepared. All I have to do is walk in and pick it up! And it better be ready!)

To be fair, I get it. Admittedly, I am guilty of many of these conveniences (and a snob when it comes to some of them if I'm being really honest). But where do we draw the line? What are we teaching our kids when we foster, demonstrate, and condone the "I want it NOW" mentality? When will we recognize that we are setting them up for failure and disappointment?

It's time to REBOOT, RESET, and RETRAIN our brains and lives.

As Dr. Michele Borba discusses in her book, *Thrivers*, we must build a generation of "thrivers", not "strivers." Kids who are "thrivers" are made, not born that way. The way to ensure this is to cultivate a spirit of resiliency by instilling balanced skills focused on managing challenges, and not merely focus on accolades, rewards, and accomplishments that result from a high GPA, cognitive hype, getting accepted into their dream school, etc. Realize that resilience is doable if we strengthen our parenting and decision making process. So, as part of the call to Reboot, Reset, and Retrain, I challenge you to look at these seven traits Dr. Borba says will help this generation become more balanced and capable of dealing with the ebbs and flows of life, including the notion that life will still be great even if their dream school rejects them.

7 Teachable Character Traits

1. Self-confidence
2. Empathy
3. Self-control

4. Integrity
5. Curiosity
6. Perseverance
7. Optimism

Learning these tools, and applying them to challenging situations (without you doing for your child what they can do for themselves) will help them immeasurably in the future. But you must reassure them and not add to the pressures they face, as well as their fear of disappointing you. So because Dr. Borga provided a great formula for parents to lead by example and therefore be a great resilience coach for their kids, I enthusiastically agree and suggest that we adopt these four steps in our process of re-evaluating how we approach college:

1. Let them know you love them no matter what.
2. Let them also know that mistakes are okay in your house.
3. Redefine success. *Real!* success is a gain.
4. Help them break down "insurmountable" tasks into small, manageable pieces.

There are certain things in life where you cannot circumvent the process. Skipping steps, half-doing steps, or eliminating them altogether will alter the outcome and not give you what you want. A principle of life and business applies here, and it's that you either pay for it now or you pay for it later; the challenge is that when you pay for it later, the cost is always higher. Life is not filled with sprints, but more of a combination of marathons, hurdles, and high jumps. Learning how to persevere with resilience is the key.

In a time where college is less affordable and yet the need to start earlier and work harder is so very necessary, we are less apt to adopt this work ethic because we've grown complacent, entitled, and apathetic about basic principles of life, such as working for what you want. I remember first hearing and, ultimately, learning the following:

- Money don't grow on trees.
- Nothing worth having will come easy.
- You must plan for what you want and work hard for it.
- The world owes you nothing.
- Nothing comes easy in life.
- Anything worth having is worth working and praying for.

I'm sure you've heard various versions of these phrases throughout your life, and have likely even applied them as well. They've now been replaced with the premise that being a great parent is giving our kids whatever they want, requiring no sacrifice on their part. If it makes the child uncomfortable...well, we don't want that to happen. Why? Because our microwave society tells us that we can be like Dorothy in the Wizard of Oz, click my heels three times, and whatever I desire will materialize.

We can no longer afford to live life as a 280-character tweet or viral TikTok video. Families are financially dying and our kids are more stressed, anxious, and prone to suffering a psychological breakdown. On top of being less prepared to tackle the curveballs of life they are sure to face economic downturns, pandemics, and job loss, among other maladies.

My challenge is for parents, mentors, grandparents, and youth leaders to commit to this paradigm shift and take the necessary steps needed to build resilient and balanced kids. By doing so, they can live out their dreams without the debt and unrealistic expectations that keep them anxious and stressed.

REEXAMINE YOUR MOTIVES AND GOALS

So, you want your child to go to college. Why?

Degree, to not degree. What about a trade?

You want them to go to your alma mater, their dream school, or a big name institution. Why?

Why is college important to your family? Is it to give your child options concerning their career and future? Does it really matter what school they attend? Is a college degree in fact the best pathway for your child?

I know, I hit you with many thought-provoking questions at the start of this book. Who does that? I guess I do, but there's a good reason for that. I want your brain to immediately start processing your *why*. Based on studies that examine the ways we think, Harvard Business Review discussed a common trap called "status quo". We inherently succumb to the biases we all carry and let them influence the decisions and choices we make. Therefore, messages and common practices we are familiar with that don't upset the apple cart are comfortable and easier to handle. The source of this thinking lies deep within our psyches as a mode of protection. If we do what is comfortable, we can avoid disappointment or damage to our ego. It ultimately becomes the safe path.

There are, however, other dangers associated with operating in a place of status quo. The law of attraction becomes a factor, as this magnetic energy of staying in a place that avoids taking a risk is prevalent, and our children are likely to adopt the same behavior. A Harvard Business Review article shares the following techniques to lessen the pull on you, your family, and your life in general:

- Always remind yourself of your objectives and examine how they would be served by the status quo.

- Never think of the status quo as your only alternative. Identify other options and use them as counterbalances, carefully evaluating all the pluses and minuses.

- Ask yourself whether you would choose the status quo alternative if, in fact, it weren't the status quo.

- Avoid exaggerating the effort or cost involved in switching from the status quo.

- Remember that the desirability of the status quo will change over time. When comparing alternatives, always evaluate them in terms of the future as well as the present.

- If you have several alternatives that are superior to the status quo, don't default to the status quo just because you're having a hard time picking the best option. Force yourself to choose.

(HBR - The Hidden Traps in Decision Making, John S. Hammond, Ralph L. Keeney, and Howard Raiffa; September-October 1998)

Also, avoiding the trap of the following notions is what I'm challenging you to break away from:

- You must have a college degree to be successful.
- You must attend a certain caliber of a college in order to make it in this life.
- Student loan debt (or even parent loan debt) is worth you attending that college regardless of the situation.
- Getting a trade is not good enough.
- Starting out at a community college is beneath you/us.
- Attending a state school is not good enough.

These are the common stories, reasons, and excuses I've heard families say to their children (or to me) when discussing dreams and aspirations for their future.

Having heard this enough and constantly seeing families intentionally go into debt because of their belief in these myths, I felt compelled to sound the alarm and challenge another part of the college admissions game.

The reality is this: real opportunity is based on the potential, finesse, wisdom, keen insight, and ability to operate strategically a person wields in the space they position themselves for. Because the answer to every problem is a person, and so identifying the right person and creatively getting connected is what it boils down to. With the internet and social media platforms, this more and more becomes an easier process.

So, let's examine what is true and actually possible.

First, I want to ask you another question.

What percentage of Fortune 100 CEOs would you say graduated from "top-tier" institutions?

There's only one Ivy League graduate in the top ten companies, and eleven total in the top 100. Most Fortune 100 CEOs didn't graduate from an Ivy League school. To be more specific, eighty-nine percent of Fortune 100 CEOs actually graduated from a non-Ivy League school. Forty-seven percent of them graduated from state schools, while the rest graduated from private institutions.

Here's a sample of some popular CEOs with degrees from non-Ivy schools.

Tim Cook, CEO of Apple (Auburn University)

Doug McMillion, CEO of Walmart (University of Arkansas)

Warren Buffett, CEO of Berkshire Hathaway (University of Nebraska Lincoln)

Mary Barra, CEO of GM (Kettering University)

The power, therefore, is not in the name of the school or the school's reputation, but rather in the power of the student's ability to:

1. Remain committed to their vision and dreams
2. Work their plan daily without giving up
3. Not get caught up the labels of the world

Whether the choice is a four-year institution, a trade, a certificate program, the military, or something entirely different, it must make sense and support your defined goals. Obtaining a college degree will not be a part of every child's story. Don't force it. You can't make a square peg fit in a round hole. Explore all viable options and be excited about their journey with them.

Parents, you play a role in helping your child understand this, and it all circles back to the previous chapter when we examined the need to build resilient students with the strategies prescribed by Dr. Michele Borba. It is a continuing theme throughout this book, and the application of the R.E.B.O.O.T. system.

To further illustrate what this looks like and to help you understand why this first part of the system is so important, I'll tell you a little about one of my clients.

Kya, a prolific blogger, writer, and seasoned educator, was very astute in the educational world and understanding its critical role in creating options and opportunities for her five children. Although she had high expectations and big dreams for her kids, there were two truths she was committed to:

1. She wouldn't cosign or greenlight student loan debt.
2. She couldn't want better for them more than they wanted it for themselves.

She took the necessary steps with her husband to support their kids' dreams, market their talents and businesses, and equip them with the skills and know-how for being successful inside and outside the classroom. They knew that their ability to take the reins over their future by maximizing the opportunities they positioned their children for was a step the kids themselves must embrace in order for it to work. She and her husband set that as the expectation and held their kids accountable to it. Some of their children embraced it more than the others. This was a challenge because Kya would have loved to have stepped in and rescued them, but what behaviors would she be fostering, and what lessons would the kids learn? Instead, she stuck to her guns and part of the positive results are still evident and even materializing today. Perhaps most poignantly, I'll share the outcome of the child and scholar she hired me to help her with.

Part of Kya's position stemmed from having had accumulated her own student loan debt that she was still paying down. She did not want the same scenario for her kids, no matter what the perceived benefits were. Her oldest started college but didn't finish, so the primary focus became her current high school senior (whom I was working with) and the junior who was next in line. Setting the stage for them to receive a debt-free education would lay the groundwork for the younger two.

We met via social media a few years prior to her becoming a client. When we first spoke about me working with her family, she shared those two truths with me and never wavered regarding her motives and goals for her kids. Not wanting her children to be married to the $1.7 trillion student loan debt crisis led to her graduating senior attending a college they could afford in a neighboring state. Not only did the school offer a credible curriculum, but it also offered in-state reciprocity because it was a connected state, thus eliminating out-of-state fees.

Incidentally, Kya's daughter also attracted over $656,000 in scholarship offers.

As you can see, there are plenty of options out there if you are open to focusing on the bigger picture of what's most important for you. Having an open mind gives you the chance to see all the opportunities that exist.

Here is what I want you to walk away with from this chapter:

It's time to get back to the basics and focus on what matters the most. This is really important and emphatically necessary. The state of getting caught up in the emotions and appearance of "I've arrived" or family traditions or doing what is "comfortable" is crippling our kids' and our families' futures. Most of the time, these kids are strapped with a lifetime of debt all because we made a long-term decision off of a temporary emotion or insecurity. The cost of flossing or staying comfortable just isn't worth it in the end.

CALL TO ACTION

Based on this chapter's learnings, answer the following questions.

What do I need to stop doing?

_____

_____

_____

_____

What do I need to start doing or do more of?

_____

_____

_____

_____

What resources am I lacking, but need to secure to aid in my success?

_____

_____

_____

_____

What is the first thing I am willing to commit to achieving?

_____

_____

_____

_____

EDUCATE YOUR BASE ON YOUR WHY

We are created *on* purpose, *for* purpose and *with* purpose. This connects to how we outline our future dreams and aspirations. It is our future, and we know the motivation behind our goals outlined in the previous chapter, so why do we let other people and naysayers have input, allow them to question us, and try to influence our why, when, and how? Instead of letting the world, family members, and others dictate the path for your life and your child's life (including the college you choose, the notion that student loan debt is worth it, etc.), walk in your power and tell them how this journey will be carried out.

Think about it. How receptive would they be if you told them how to spend their paycheck each pay period? They wouldn't welcome your opinions, especially if you said something like, "You can use your rent or mortgage money to pay for this vacation. Paying late won't hurt anything because you deserve to take the vacation of your dreams." Your mortgage company or landlord can't take your desires to unwind over to the bank and cash it. They want their money. So why would you allow others who aren't footing the bill or contributing to the cause to dictate the type of college your child should attend or how signing for his loan will pay off in the future?

This is where you must embody your motives and let the goals identified in the first chapter become your speaking points for setting boundaries on how your family will move, act, and go forward regarding the direction of your child's future. The reality is this: more adults are burdened with student debt than ever before. Don't believe me? Take these statistics, for example from the U.S. Department of Education, National Center for Education Statistics. Thirty-two years ago in 1989, student loan debt was only 8 percent. Fast forward to present day, the number of households with student loan debt has tripled. When you segregate the data and look at younger households, you see similar trends. The Federal Reserve and the U.S. Department of Education says younger families with student loan debt increased from 15 percent to 41 percent over the same period. Because more families are feeding the $1.7 trillion debt crisis, there is a correlation towards purchasing categories like homeownership. Crippling debt is prohibiting more young adults from affording a home. Over a 9-year period from 2005 to 2014, reports say there was a decline in homeownership of 4 percent, but the rate for those between the ages of 25 and 34 fell 9 percent. Consequently, more youth moved back home to live with mommy, daddy, and grandparents because of their inability to live on their own.

Is this worth it?

The amount of debt owed in present day is substantially greater than it was when I came out of college in 1998. At that time, students graduated with their degrees and on average $14,590 in student loan debt. Today, on average, college graduates leave with their diplomas and $39,351 in student loan debt; a 170 percent increase. We cannot ignore these numbers and the trends these past decades, along with the fact that more students are borrowing than ever before. (U.S. Dept. of Education, National Center for Education Statistics)

Another alarming trend I must point out is the alarming number of loans in default or delinquent before COVID. The number of loans in default or delinquency status was already rising prior to the pandemic. The amount of loans increased nearly 50 percent—rising from $178 billion in 2016 to $263 billion in early 2020. (U.S. Dept. of Education, National Center for Education Statistics)

These stats should be very troubling, and are part of my motivation for writing this book. Not enough discussions about the true impact of debt are taking place, especially within Black and Hispanic households, where the most impact is felt the deepest.

Every time I presented a college workshop on how to pay for college at expos across the country, I would ask parents, "How many of you would be excited about your child coming back home after moving out?" Then I would ask the students, "How excited are you about moving back home with mom and dad after being out on your own?" Neither group was thrilled about these concepts. As a matter of fact, they overwhelmingly responded with how much of a bad idea it would be. If this is true, why are we scared to make the hard decisions required to mitigate and prevent it from happening?

I'm not entirely sure. But I am here to challenge you to take the leap and make the hard decision. To do that, you must establish the ground rules, stick to them and hold everyone else to them as well. These are the days of your life, and also of your child's life. When it comes to the statistics shared earlier and the financial implications, you should be in the driver's seat and consider the true cost of every decision.

Because I know this can be hard, I am going to share with you another story of one of many ways to achieve this in real life. We can get the same message from Kya's story in the previous chapter, but I want to add some ammunition to this fire with Ms. Andrea's story.

A few years back, I was speaking at a youth event and our paths crossed. From there, we continued to be in the same space and eventually connected when I facilitated a workshop for the mentoring organization Andrea worked with. If you knew Ms. Andrea like I do, you would fall in love with her and forever keep her in your life. She has the most beautiful spirit, and is inspiring and motivating. She truly cares about young people and, like me, she considers all of them her babies. I would say that this is one of the many reasons we connected.

Andrea researched and provided resources and tips for the students in her program and community. Then the time came for her to apply her learnings to her pride and joy and the apple of her eye; her only daughter (and also her "mini me"). Naturally, her concern as a mom was real and not unfounded when it came to the effects of student loan debt and its crippling trends. She felt she wouldn't be doing her job if she didn't have a hard conversation with her daughter and establish the right boundaries for this next phase of life. Ms. Andrea and her husband didn't have the financial means to just write a check; most families don't. But going into debt for a degree wasn't an option. It was especially true that the income to be earned in her chosen career field would not be commensurate with the cost to where it could be paid off in less than ten years. It just didn't make financial sense. Ms. Andrea had to get ready for the "big talk." We like to think of the "big talk" as being about sex, but there are multiple similarly huge conversations we must contend with in today's time.

The talk couldn't be prolonged any longer because of the conversations between her daughter and her girlfriends, where they began to brag about college, name dropping schools on their list considered to be the more "prestigious" academic institutions. Granted, the conversations were all about attending these schools and them being the only options and so forth, but nobody had the means to cover the full bill, let alone a third of it. Setting her baby girl up for a major let down was on the horizon and she had to control the narrative and set realistic expectations.

Of course, she and her husband want their daughter to have the same opportunity as her friends, but they knew it wasn't a viable option. The time finally came for the "big talk." They sat her down and began to explain how the economic downturn had changed the trajectory of their family and the sacrifices they had to make to stay afloat. Part of growing up is being responsible and making hard decisions, they told her. As much as they would love for her to pick the school of her choice and hand her a large check to cover it, it just wasn't going to happen. The cost of paying now versus later is a lesson to master now, they explained. They proceeded to outline how college could be a viable option without sacrificing their soul and entire life by signing on to the amount of debt her friends were going to take on for the schools they were pursuing. Although their approach was not a popular one, a non-traditional path that took slightly longer, the end result would still reign true: a degree from an accredited program with zero debt. This dream came true, as their baby girl walked across that stage this year debt free. Meanwhile, her friends graduated earlier with a boatload of debt and financial stress.

CALL TO ACTION

The power of telling our kids "no" is necessary and does not make you a bad parent. Remember: we are cultivating resilient children who are thrivers, equipped to become our future leaders, judges, presidents, CEOs, and so forth. You can't have them thinking that everything in life comes easy, that sacrifice is not a way of life and that there are no costs or ramifications of our actions. This approach sets them up for failure and mental anguish, likely for the rest of their lives. This is why I am sharing these tools, tactics, and resources with you. The resource I'd like to introduce here is the book, *No: Why Kids—of All Ages—Need to Hear It and Ways Parents Can Say It*. This book was a welcomed addition to my library after hearing countless families over the years say, "It's their choice, and I will make the necessary sacrifices for them to attend their dream school." There goes that phrase again. You will eventually see I am so over this notion of the so-called dream school being the *only* school.

But in Dr. Walsh's book, he helps us understand the logic and science behind why our kids do what they do at different stages of life. If we are being honest with ourselves, we have evolved into a society of acceptance, intolerance, "yes" over "no", "me, me, me", "more", "fast", and "fun". This is why we need to apply his practical tools and instill a level of self-discipline as parents that will carry on further within our kids. The sad reality is that children in the U.S. are falling drastically behind kids from other countries on a global scale. We combat this by recognizing the heavy lift in owning that the real learning happens on our watch at home, outside of the classroom. It is <u>our</u> responsibility, not the school's. Just like it's not the school's responsibility to raise and teach our kids about life, it's also not its job to get them college and career ready. Are you ready to reclaim your role in constructing your child's future?

Based on this chapter's learnings, answer the following questions.

What is my "why"? Describe it in detail.

_____

_____

_____

_____

What do I need to stop doing?

_____

_____

_____

_____

What do I need to start doing or do more of?

_____

_____

_____

_____

What resources am I lacking, but need to secure to aid in my success?

_____

_____

_____

_____

What is the first thing I am willing to commit to achieving?

_____

_____

_____

_____

BEGIN WITH THE END IN MIND AND WORK BACKWARDS

I've always said that you can take the girl out of engineering, but you can't take the engineer out the girl. I am a scientist at heart, always focused on solving problems and looking for ways to improve processes. This chapter is rooted in reverse engineering your final destination and mapping out sustainable steps to get you there and in a space of happiness, fulfillment and success.

Using short-sighted views to select a college is like dating the wrong person. I recently posted a quote of mine that said: "Selecting the wrong college and committing to student loan debt is like being in a relationship with a person who just isn't that into you." Think about it: one-sided relationships are temporal and tend to end in heartbreak. The love (infatuation, rather) we feel compromises our ability to think about the long-term effects. Falling victim to those feel-good emotions lead to us later discovering we didn't fully get what we needed or expected out of that relationship. Relating this to selecting a college based on surface reasons and various emotions (some perhaps misguided) will only last until we start feeling the effects of paying those student loan payments each month and the need to skip on that shopping trip or vacation because we don't have enough money to make ends meet. Skipping on student loan payments will lead to bad credit and garnished paychecks and possibly no tax refunds, which will further limit how we live our lives after getting that degree from the college that gave us bragging rights and the ability to floss on social media.

Again, I ask: is it worth it?

"Begin with the End in Mind" comes from the highly acclaimed leadership book on personal change, *"The 7 Habits of Highly Effective People"* by Steven. R. Covey. In the book, there are many jewels and nuggets such as writing your own mission statement, philosophy, or creed because it enables you to focus on what you want to be (character) and what you want to do (contributions and achievements). This ties into his recommendation to write your own epitaph. This may sound morbid, but it helps us to reflect on our legacy and what we want it to look like. At your funeral, what would you like to be said about you? What traits would you like people to use in describing you? I challenge you to apply this to your child. What descriptors would you use to describe the type of future you want them to have? What are some of the things you couldn't afford to have when you were their age, and would you like for them to experience? What are the things you've

experienced or are still experiencing that are crippling your vision for a life you would like to protect them from?

Answering these questions is your start to beginning with the end in mind. So, take the time to become quiet and answer those questions. Once you do, you will be in a position to break each of them down into steps and pieces on how to get your child to that desired result and state, whether it's the kind of person they become, a class, training, experience, or a combination of everything.

If you are feeling stuck and need an example of how to initiate this process, I'll give you another example of a family and their situation. Before I do that, a bit more context on what this chapter is all about.

It's easy to get side-tracked and frustrated because of all the moving pieces and layers involved with getting college and career ready, going through the application process, and then getting it paid for. You must have focused energy and time towards driving this process. Making a wrong move in this game can result in lost opportunities, cost you tens or even hundreds of thousands of dollars, or lead you down an endless path that doesn't yield any positive dividends. It reminds me of Sam Chand's books, *"Who Moved Your Ladder?"*, *"What's Shaking Your Ladder?"*, and *"Ladder Shifts"*. If your ladder is in the wrong place or leaning up against the wrong wall, every step up that ladder will get you to the wrong destination and result in multiple restarts. This leads to more confusion. If you don't have the right guidance or focus, you will find yourself constantly getting the same results. Plenty of movement, but nothing accomplished.

Next, let's learn about the path of future doctor Mia and her mom Marcella.

Marcella knew she had to come up with a solid college plan her family could live up to with two daughters graduating from high school two years apart. This meant they would both be in college at the same time and the oldest daughter, whom I have worked with, was going on to become a doctor. This made the desire for a debt-free education that much more paramount.

The end result included getting the oldest daughter, Mia, through medical school with minimum debt and both undergraduate degrees paid for. Having a clear vision of their destination, Marcella made the conscious decision to procure my services as a valued resource to help actualize her vision for her family. After partnering and developing a strategy for the next nine years, Marcella and Mia immediately got to work. The system they created for their family was like an assembly line at a manufacturing company. They were armed with structured and timely hand-offs between stages that resulted in Mia earning over one million dollars in scholarships and, ultimately, selecting a college where everything was paid for.

I want to point out something about the decision they made as a family regarding the school they selected. This was not a school on their wish list. It was a school introduced to them based on the final destination and vision Marcella had articulated to me in our early meetings. She and Mia stayed true to how they saw their end result, which allowed them to be open to every opportunity presented to them. Now Mia is thriving, working the relationships she established, and things are looking promising on her journey to getting medical school covered. The lessons and resources garnered for Mia's journey were applied to Marcella's youngest daughter. It created the pathway for her younger scholar to also attend college without being burdened with extensive debt.

Again, the best choice is not in the name or ranking of the school, but in your approach and the abilities of your student. What adjustments are you willing to make in helping to guide your child up the right ladder? Those adjustments will lead to real and sustainable opportunities that support that bold vision you initially wanted to see manifested in your child's future.

CALL TO ACTION

Based on this chapter's learnings, answer the following questions.

What does the final destination look like?

_____

_____

_____

_____

What is needed to reach my final destination?

_____

_____

_____

_____

What resources am I lacking to reach that destination?

_____

_____

_____

_____

What does success look like?

_____

_____

_____

_____

OUTLINE YOUR STEPS FORWARD

Being able to pay for college is a game and a massive process that oftentimes equates to an ant trying to eat and swallow an elephant. Some may have a hard time imagining this, but it is possible for an ant to eat an elephant in theory. They do it one bite at a time. However, those bites are the result of understanding how the game is played. Let's relate that to the trials of paying for college education: one needs to determine the best way to slice and dice this massive animal, in this case college finances, into ant-sized pieces.

Learning how to R.E.B.O.O.T requires a level of discipline with preparation and planning. I recall learning early in my career the 5 Ps. I loved the concept so much that I later incorporated it into various leadership and project management training classes I taught around the country. Here's what the 5 Ps stand for:

Proper planning prevents poor performance.

As a project management professional, planning is the most crucial step in any process when it comes to initiative, goal, aspiration, and so forth. If you don't plan your steps, how will you know where to start, when to start, who to include or exclude, or even the things you require to start? This rings true for the college admissions process. It is not the college admissions of the early nineties. Today's process is so much more convoluted, with varying loopholes, traps, and landmines. If you don't know how to play the game and navigate around those time-wasters, those rim and front-end destroying potholes, the path to a debt-free education is almost impossible. Parents must learn the art of proper planning and preparation.

Using what you outlined at the end of the previous chapters, you should now at least be able to get off of home base, get into the game, and define the intricate steps needed to move your family around the bases without striking out. But you can't be afraid to get in the game, put it on paper, test your processes, and make the adjustments where necessary. Think of a batter looking to connect with the ball and secure a spot on one of the bases, if not a home run. A skilled player will examine how the pitcher delivered previous balls to ascertain how they need to adjust their stance, swing, and gauge of readiness to time when to swing so that a fruitful connection is made. This is how I want you to think about the college and career-ready process and the role the R.E.B.O.O.T system plays in it.

Just as I tell the students in my project management classes at the university, as well as the professional leaders who take my PMP Bootcamps: processes are all around us. They are something we innately do without thinking about it. We plan our kids' first birthday party, their graduation parties, our retirement parties and family vacations. At the end of the day, they are all what we would define in the project management space as a "process." The same definition applies to planning for college. With it being such a massive undertaking, you should break it up into the following four phases, and then break those phases up into smaller tasks:

- Pre-staging phase: this covers birth to fifth grade. It is where we lay the groundwork for establishing a savings plan, cultivate our vocabulary, reading comprehension, study skills, and the discipline of delivering quality work and products.

- Elevate phase: this covers the sixth to eighth grades. In this phase, you are taking the learnings and the mindset established in the previous stage to the next level. Your child is challenged more with exposure to time management basics, more rigorous coursework, and greater responsibilities to manage. Their mindset should shift from *tell* me how to do it to *coach* me how to do it, ending with them being able to handle it themselves at the next phase.

- Execution phase: these are the high school years, and what happens here will directly dictate the options and opportunities available to your child come their senior year. The stronger they navigate through the previous stages, the more prepared they will be to fully lead and own their process and journey of becoming. The key at this stage is being resilient and self-sufficient in knowing how to seek help, drive their own accomplishments, demonstrate selfless and leadership abilities, and have a sense of direction about their future.

- Promotion phase: this is the last stage of this cycle, and spans your child's college years. Students are now independent of their parents and should be capable of promoting their own ideas, beliefs, and expectations. They are in the driver's seat with the power to set the pace, define the course, and identify who goes with them on their journey into the professional world and life in general.

There is a major prerequisite for being able to map out all four phases into bite-sized pieces. Remember the previous chapter, "*Begin with the End in Mind*"? You can't visualize or define something you can't identify. That final destination must be known before completing the steps in this chapter. If your child is lacking in this area, that is okay. They now have an opportunity to go on a journey of self-discovery and find a pathway they can get excited about. Your help, guidance, and support is needed here, at minimum.

In my practice, I've been fortunate to engage with some awesome youth across the world. One that stands out to me is a client of mine, Keala.

A few years later, it was a sunny and warm day in June when I pulled up in front of the family's home. They scheduled their strategy session with me a few days before going back to Asia, as they were one of the families we worked with that year who lived overseas. How cool is that? I never would've imagined living in another country during my high school years. Excelling in that type of environment requires a certain level of charisma, discipline, big-picture thinking, and leadership. Keala had all of these qualities and many more. She was one of the most articulate, outgoing, and charismatic scholars I have ever had the opportunity of coaching. When I think of ways to describe this future International Business Leader, I would say goal-oriented, driven by vision, determined, focused in her approach, results-driven, analytical, and process-driven. Her mode of operating reminds me of an elite military leader on a recon mission, mapping out how to conquer their next mission. She operated with a keen sense of wisdom beyond her years.

Comparing Keala to adults I've coached, managed, or trained, she certainly had better decision making, problem-solving, and analytical skills than many of them. The type of wisdom she exuded was akin to that of Solomon in the Bible. Along with that wisdom, she was very mature for her age group. When I think about what a student would need to succeed at living abroad, she had all of the right qualities. It must be noted that her mom was actively involved. Because Keala epitomized every quality of a leader, her mom was comfortable assisting on the side.

Ultimately, like any great leader, she estimated the college landscape. She planned how to move forward, defined her needs, assigned tasks and roles, established a plan of action based on the mission and her customized strategy, executed everything beautifully, tracked the results, and made adjustments according to negotiated results. This led her to being in the best position to overcome the effects of COVID and still have a masterful school year virtually.

Bear in mind that I have illustrated how Keala killed the college game and made decisions that made dollars and cents for her family because she remained committed to the other parts of the R.E.B.O.O.T. model. But that's not how we started. Keala wasn't always excited about the process. Once she learned the basic construct of the college admissions game and how it should be played, she shifted and adjusted how she moved forward. Nobody likes to change their plan, especially when money has been invested and your emotions are tied to the results.

Remember, Keala had wisdom beyond her years. She was organized and prepared. Yes, she executed calculated moves, but they were based on her limited knowledge of the college preparation process. Like most families, she was clueless that the process really was a game and a massive maze designed to chew you up and spit you out if you're not careful. So when she proudly walked me through how she compiled her top ten list, had mapped out and executed her visits to these schools, and relayed the final result of who made the cut and who didn't, it was like I took all the wind out of her sails when I revealed data about the final list. Keala was deflated, as the life seemed to leave her highly energetic body. She began to feel a range of emotions associated with being disappointed because the actions taken in her mind were a waste of time and money. Having mom spend money unnecessarily was not something Keala wanted. Upon seeing this, I gave her a different perspective and it expanded her mind to see the glass half full as opposed to half empty.

I encouraged her to take her analysis and detailed notes about each school and repurpose them. The problem with her initial list was the fact that the schools' funding models would not give her what she needed financially to attend and graduate. You see, we can't solely look at the emotional and feel-good elements of a school and make a decision based on them alone. Logic and a reality check are needed to produce sustainable outcomes. Once Keala realized all was not lost in having to scrap her list and start over to get a new group of colleges that met her funding requirements, she didn't let the disappointment hold her hostage. Instead, she became like a duck, letting the water bead up on her back and roll off. She had to keep it moving because there was work to do.

Making hard and challenging decisions makes adulting quite unattractive to young adults, but it's part of maturing and growing up. This was Keala's opportunity to learn the lesson and get in position to do it again, as it is the essence of the college admissions and funding process. Her mom, of course, was fully engaged throughout the entire process and was there to fill in those gaps and reaffirm her where it was needed.

Too often, parents won't do this, and instead take the friend approach, letting their kids make this crucial decision on their own that oftentimes lands them as a family in a lifetime of suffocating debt. If you don't believe me, go back to the statistics shared in the beginning of the book. Alternatively, you can glean from a conversation and proposed partnership with insurance and financial advisors.

A former colleague who has her own agency solicited my help with her clients because the trend of families and their inability to retire and invest became more prevalent. These families pulled equity from their homes, withdrew money from their retirement, and/or took on Parent PLUS loans to make their kids' college dreams a reality. On the other end, her clients couldn't afford to save early in their careers and didn't qualify for home loans because they had too much student loan debt. Being a planner, she wanted to be proactive by identifying solutions for families she could help to avoid getting into similar situations.

But back to Keala for a moment. She traveled back to Asia with a game plan she executed beautifully. She embraced the terms of the game, made her plays, and maximized every opportunity. So much so that her advocating and negotiation skills produced multiple increases in various financial aid packets. Also, and here's the kicker: the school she ended up at gave her more money than was offered to two of our other scholars vying for higher packages at the same institution who had higher GPAs and ACT scores than Keala.

When you have the confidence and training, there is no stopping you from accomplishing your goals.

CALL TO ACTION

Based on this chapter's learnings, answer the following questions.

What do I need to stop doing?

_____

_____

_____

_____

What do I need to start doing or do more of?

_____

_____

_____

_____

What resources am I lacking, but need to secure to aid in my success?

_____

_____

_____

_____

What is the first thing I am willing to commit to achieving?

_____

_____

_____

_____

ORCHESTRATE THE RIGHT DREAM TEAM

"The key, answer, or solution to every problem is a person."

"Your net worth is only as good as your network."

"Teamwork makes the dream work."

And the list goes on. These are a few phrases I've been told and have used myself when discussing the power of having a dream team. Every successful person has a tribe. Without one, you would be doing life alone, and probably going nowhere. This is not how life was meant to be lived. Everyone needs a circle of people to inspire, coach, or guide them and bounce things off of. The key here is selecting the right people. A person close enough to help is also close enough to harm you. It may not be something you would think of in the space of college and career readiness, but you should. Unfortunately, there are people in this space that give bad information, sharing untruths and outdated data. Listening to them and following their misguided advice can cost you money, time, connections, and opportunities.

"We cannot solve our problems with the same thinking we used when we created them."

—Albert Einstein

"Teamwork makes the dream work, but a vision becomes a nightmare when the leader has a big dream and a bad team."

—John C. Maxwell

The key here is being open to receiving help and then selecting the best person to fill the job. You must know what your gaps and needs are in order to do this effectively. Think of a sports team leading up to draft season. A great coach identifies its weak points and starts making moves to negotiate side deals, trades, and scout out new talents. I played basketball and like to use it to teach leadership lessons, so I will use it here as an analogy.

A basketball team is comprised of the following positions (and since I played the game myself, I can relate!):

1. Center (my position): the tallest player on the team, playing near the basket. Their role is to score on close shots and rebound on offense.

But on defense, the goal is to block the opponents' shots and rebound their misses.

2. Power Forward: similar to the role of center, except they also take longer range shots than centers.

3. Small Forward: a versatile position, because they play against both small and large players, roam all over the court, and have the ability to score from long and close shots.

4. Point Guard: usually the team's best dribbler and passer, who oftentimes sets the pace of the game in how they call plays under the coach's direction. They defend the opponent's point guard and look for opportunities to steal the ball and force a turnover.

5. Shooting Guard: usually the team's best shooter, making shots from long distance with often very good dribbling skills.

In the process of getting college and career ready, there are many key roles that can add value to your process. Here are some key positions to consider:

- Career Coach or Counselor: they can provide insight about viable career paths, requirements, changing demographics, etc. Also, they can be the connection point towards internship, enrichment, and scholarship opportunities.

- College Coach or Professional: they are subject matter experts skilled with the knowledge, the training and inside track on what's needed to get into college.

- High School Counselor: their role is to help students get through high school. They are not experts in the college admissions and scholarship space, having limited depth of knowledge on how to advise students beyond the bare basics.

- Tutor or Academic Coach: they are subject matter experts on one or more academic areas where they can teach, coach, and guide students on how to perform at a higher level.

- Mentor: they can bring the balance and creative insight students need, enabling them to properly manage the stresses of life and have an outlet they trust independent of the family.

- Cheerleader: this person is your chief encourager and motivator. During the stressful moments you are bound to encounter, you will need this person to remind you that "you can do it" and "don't give up."

- Other Parents: they are essential. Knowing you are not alone helps. Connecting with other parents who are either going through, already went through, or are about to go through the same experience can be advantageous to all. Information is shared, tips and strategies are passed along, and outlets abound to vent frustrations about a very convoluted and stressful process.

- Career Professionals: they are different from Career Coaches because they are directly in the field and provide more insight in real time regarding job trends, opportunities, ways to prepare, etc.

- College Professionals: these are professionals who work at an institution familiar with the school's admissions and scholarship process. They can also share other opportunities available that might be of interest when picking the right schools.

- Prayer Person: they can help to ground you and to focus on positive perspectives. Regardless of your religious beliefs, having a spiritual focus never hurts.

This is not an exhaustive list, but one you can start with when building your dream team. When I reflect on the basketball roles I've had and applied them here, my area of genius was in being a solid post-player, AKA the Center. Operating in that area makes me inefficient in the other roles. Therefore, I have a tribe of people in my inner circle to fill the gaps I'm not skilled at. Not only do I have some shooting and point guards, power and small forwards, I also have a few coaches and cheerleaders. I'm not telling you to do something I've researched. These are tactics I do personally in my life and business, as well as with my clients.

Remember that college admissions is a game. You need to surround yourself with the right people to aid you in navigating the waters of college admissions and funding. I can't stress it enough: doing it alone has left families bewildered, confused, and extremely stressed. You see this playing out on thousands of posts made on social media weekly. Don't let this be you. Combat this is by finding like-minded people with similar spirits, interests, discipline, and the same accountability as you. It won't work if it's a one-sided relationship.

Remember the hopeful family from the introduction? Their daughter was the star student with no money for school and limited school options. Because they bought into the hype of the myth that honor roll students would have limited money and opportunities, they were left holding the bag of disappointment, anxiety, stress, confusion, and frustration. When they reached out to their network and became connected with me, it was at the eleventh hour. Imagine the number of opportunities this scholar with a 4.3+ GPA and 1300+ SAT score could've had if they had tapped into their network sooner and sought my help in the beginning. They could have possibly garnered a similar outcome to one of our scholars, who had similar scores and attracted over $2.5 million in scholarships from top-tiered institutions.

The process works. You just have to know how to make it work for you and find the solutions to your problems in the form of people.

CALL TO ACTION

Based on this chapter's learnings, answer the following questions.

What do I need to stop doing?

_____

_____

_____

_____

What do I need to start doing or do more of?

_____

_____

_____

_____

What gaps in resources or knowledge am I lacking, but need to facilitate my process?

_____

_____

_____

_____

What ten people can you list who can be an asset to your Dream Team?

_____

_____

_____

_____

TRACK, MONITOR, AND CONTROL THE JOURNEY

You made it to the last step in rebooting, resetting, and retraining your mind, and the views and approaches of how we do college. No approach, system, or process is perfect; they all have an element of experimentation. When you experiment, you do something, you check the results and then you act on what those results reveal. This is essentially the idea behind this step in the process.

To properly gauge whether or not goals are met, the steps taken align with goals and the final destination, and everything is in sync with the outlined steps, everything must be documented, tracked, results and impact monitored, and then controlled by editing it along the way to ensure your desired outcomes are reached. You must be organized and have a system to avoid frustration and burnout. Here are some tips for getting this off the ground. Because I am a project manager and an executive leader, these are second nature for me. What I am sharing are some best practices.

- Plan and organize your time: use your big picture (goals and motives) as the destination and break down your goals, objectives, desires, and aspirations associated with it to define the necessary steps. Make sure your steps are manageable. Then organize them into a timeline or bucket of tasks and responsibilities based on what makes sense.

- Visually represent your plan: it's impossible to manage something you can't see. Take the planned and organized details and convert them into visual imaging. You can easily implement it using old-school tactics, post-it notes on flip charts, writing it in a notebook or journal, or finding software applications like Microsoft Office Suite products, Slack, Trello, monday.com, and a host of others.

- Track progress: this is where you document the current status of your tasks, goals, and targets. Have you started, is it on time, late, almost late, etc. Like the previous step, it can be done manually or using some of the tools listed in addition to other platforms like Teamweek, Toggl, Workotter, etc.

- Look for accountability: share your plan and details with your Dream Team. Then establish a meeting and reporting cadence to allow for regular check-ins and status updates. This will help you stay focused on the big picture.

- Define celebratory moments: self-motivation and encouragement to keep going comes when you celebrate accomplishments. Take the time to define how you will celebrate small wins, segments of a goal being completed, full completion, and reaching milestones.

Plan your work, then work your plan. Having a system in place and staying true to it will lead you to successful outcomes. Know that these are just ideas and not the only way. I believe in identifying what works best for you and your family. With that, I must share one more story of a client who embodied this and continues to work the process daily and win big as a college student.

I'll tell you about Tamela and her daughter Danae. As I think about their story, I just smile and my spirit is filled with joy because I am super proud of what they've done and continue to do. Yes, this is an ongoing process. So, get ready and get used to it.

Tamela is an educator, mom, grandmother, entrepreneur, wife, and motivator. She is an engaged parent who plans and strategizes everything. What she accomplished with Danae is a best practice model to be emulated, and one I share with my other clients to motivate them.

Tamela read my book, deconstructed it and outlined what she needed to do to position Danae for success after high school. Danae is a multi-talented young lady passionate about Science, Technology, Engineering and Mathematics (STEM). I see her making headlines in the future as a STEM leader in the world of computer science. Keep an eye out, she is going to be on magazine covers and highlighted in STEM-related journals and magazines. I can brag on my scholars and families all day and it gives me joy to do so.

As a great leader, she enjoys giving back by imparting knowledge and wisdom unto those who follow. Even though she is a high school student, these qualities have resulted in her creating a nonprofit focused on teaching girls how to code. Danae's organization was no fly by night initiative. She worked it consistently and created many projects and challenges. One year, she set and exceeded a goal of training 1,000 young girls on how to code. Because of her leadership, she received recognition and garnered the support of some corporate sponsors. All of this was accomplished before she was sixteen years of age. Can you see why I am proud of her and beaming with such joy as I share her story? But the pride doesn't end there.

When Tamela brought me in to coach Danae on her college plan and strategy, we discovered that she possessed enough credit hours to graduate a year early. And, as you can imagine, that's what happened. Losing a year of time to work with, and adding further exasperation to an already stressful process. The need to find enough scholarships became their top priority, but it couldn't be the only one because of the many steps needed to complete the complicated admissions process. But when I say they knocked it out the park, that would be an understatement. They did so well because of the tactics outlined in the book. They are a living example of the steps that make up the R.E.B.O.O.T. system. She did more during this time that some have done in a few years. Calculated and intentional steps pay higher dividends every time.

Remember, Danae made a decision to graduate one year early. That caused goals and key milestones to be shifted forward in the new accelerated plan. In project management, we refer to this as fast tracking the project. When you do that, you run the risk of missing key pieces, rework, too many cooks in the kitchen, and higher costs. Well, Tamela and Danae set a goal to find, apply, and win $50,000 in private scholarships. This is beyond what any school would offer her because she had the smarts and portfolio that made her a serious money magnet. Not only did Danae hit the goal, she exceeded the goal with total earnings in her freshman year of $67,000. This incredible sum was amassed because they met weekly, tracked and monitored their progress, quickly identified when they needed to shift and make adjustments, and executed and re-assessed again to ensure it all worked. Continuing to work through these repetitive iterations consistently paid off in a major way.

Danae is now a junior in college and running multiple businesses on top of working her second or third internship. Although she has all these great things on her calendar, she continues to dedicate Sundays to scholarships with her mom and a few friends she's brought along the journey as accountability partners. As a result, $90,000 was accumulated in scholarships her sophomore year, and her junior year is already looking incredibly prosperous as well. Maybe it would drive the point home even further by mentioning that she also receives a refund check each semester. Now THAT is how you do college.

There is nothing you can't do if you set your mind to it and have a solid plan and team in place to make it happen.

CALL TO ACTION

Based on this chapter's learnings, answer the following questions.

What do I need to stop doing?

_____

_____

_____

_____

What do I need to start doing or do more of?

_____

_____

_____

_____

What resources am I lacking, but need to secure to aid in my success?

_____

_____

_____

_____

What is the first thing I am willing to commit to achieving?

_____

_____

_____

_____

R.E.B.O.O.T. THE ROAD TO TRANSFORMATION

My desire to see all families succeed is unending. As painful as it is when I can't help them, I have also had to realize that I can't want it more than they want it for themselves. Yes, there are many systemic issues with our educational system that impacts kids of color more negatively. But we can't let that be the song we sing.

After seeing the same pattern of behavior over the years, I would wrack my brain trying to come up with ways to help families drowning with the logistics of cost. I already mentioned that I am a natural born problem solver. It's just who I am and how my engineering brain works. In the spirit of one of those brainstorming sessions I do with myself in my head (me and God), the concept for this book was born. R.E.B.O.O.T systematically formalized an approach I've used for years, now packaged as a practical formula of transforming our mindset and consciousness regarding how we do, view, and approach college. This is my way of sounding the alarm.

WAKE UP!!! WAKE UP!!! WAKE UP!!! WAKE UP!!!

The steps taken within the last decade aren't working when you go back and look at statistics surrounding student loan debt. Our modus operandi in this country has been that of insanity. The very definition of insanity is doing the same thing over and over again, but expecting a different result. This has been us as a people for a long time, and it is why I insist we are in a state of emergency as a country and as a family.

It's time to stop abrogating your responsibility of preparing your child for post-secondary success to the schools and counselors. As you've learned, this is not their job. Accept the challenge and the role by resetting your mind on what you knew about college, retrain and gain an understanding of the new game to connect with winning strategies, then reboot and restart with renewed hope about what you now know that can be applied in today's environment.

From the mouth of babes, wisdom speaks. One of my scholars (and future doctor, for certain) said this in her testimonial video (she earned over $2 million in award funding and is currently on full scholarship).

"…Coach Tameka is the expert, but it's up to you to take the process, own it, and run with it. By the end of your journey, you will be able to see how your diligence, your endurance, and your persistence paid off…literally."

I am challenging you to do with this book what my young scholar is advising you to do. She is not simply telling you something that she heard. She is telling you what she did to produce her desired outcome.

The choice is yours. How will you dare to change the outcome of your future destination? I want you to reflect on the chapters and think about what R.E.B.O.O.T looks like for your family and transforming your mind.

Recap: How will you:

1. Reexamine your motives and goals?
2. Educate your base on your WHY?
3. Begin with the end in mind and work backwards?
4. Outline your steps forward?
5. Orchestrate the right dream team?
6. Track, monitor, and control the journey?

Get busy today and choose to start now. How you move forward will impact your child's mental capacity, financial profile, confidence level, and so much more. Teach and show them the way, then empower them to lead.

Notes, Actions, and Tasks

Notes, Actions, and Tasks

ABOUT THE AUTHOR

Tameka L. Williamson is a passionate and dedicated motivational speaker, coach, and executive leadership strategist. She is the multi-award-winning and bestselling author of *Parents, Send Your Child to College for Free*; *Getting A Full Ride*; and *A Road to Success: The College Planning and Preparatory Guide*, as well as a contributor to two influential faith-based and educational collaborations. Her gifts run the veritable gamut when it comes to teaching academic hopefuls and their parents how to "Kill The College Game" with her insightful, groundbreaking, and revolutionary approach.

Tameka has been featured in *Forbes*, *Huffington Post*, *The Examiner*, and *Lifetime Moms*, among many other respected publications. Her life's passion is focused on improving the lives of students and leaders by connecting them to pathways of upward mobility so they can live their best lives personally and professionally. She lives in Atlanta, Georgia.

Learn more at www.tamekawilliamson.com

CREATING DISTINCTIVE BOOKS
WITH INTENTIONAL RESULTS

We're a collaborative group of creative masterminds with a mission to produce high-quality books to position you for monumental success in the marketplace.

Our professional team of writers, editors, designers, and marketing strategists work closely together to ensure that every detail of your book is a clear representation of the message in your writing.

Want to know more?
Write to us at info@publishyourgift.com
or call (888) 949-6228

Discover great books, exclusive offers, and more at
www.PublishYourGift.com

Connect with us on social media

@publishyourgift

www.ingramcontent.com/pod-product-compliance
Lightning Source LLC
Chambersburg PA
CBHW071911070526
44583CB00016B/1940